APOSTLES:

BY

CYNTHIA ALVAREZ

PUBLISHED *by* PARABLES
Earthly Stories with a Heavenly Meaning

_____

Apostles
Cynthia Alvarez

Published By Parables
February, 2019

ISBN 978-1-945698-97-2
Printed in the United States of America

Readers should be aware that Internet Web sites offered as citations and/or sources for further information may have been changed or disappeared between the time this was written and the time it is read.

APOSTLES:

BY

CYNTHIA ALVAREZ

PUBLISHED by PARABLES
Earthly Stories with a Heavenly Meaning

CONTENTS

Chapter One
Who Are God's Apostles?
Page 5

Chapter Two
Why Do We Need Apostles?
Page 17

Chapter Three
The Realm of Apostles
Page 23

Chapter Four
What Is Significant About the Work of Apostles?
Page 33

Chapter Five
The Power and Authority Invested in Apostles
Page 43

Chapter Six
Apostles and Prophets....
Page 59

Chapter Seven
The Relationship of God and His Apostles
Page 69

Cynthia Alvarez

PREFACE

The spiritual winds of change for the Body of Christ have arrived, as the Apostles of the Lord God are being ushered from obscurity and escorted to the world's center stage by the sovereign will of God. No longer can they remain hidden from the influential spheres of culture, but they must rise and take dominion of every realm of authority in the earth, which means they will need a powerful global body of believers to accomplish an undertaking of such magnitude. Not only must they have a global body of believers, but these believers must be strategically positioned in every influential sphere of culture in the earthly realm. With success in mind, Apostles clearly understand their first goal is to build and equip the Body of Christ to be a mighty end-time army for the Lord. Every soldier in this army must be groomed with expansive knowledge of the King and His Kingdom for no one to lack the truth that is found only in Christ. Once the knowledge of Christ is imparted to the body, every man will be able to take his rightful seat of authority in the influential spheres of culture while Christ rules through their hearts and minds. Then and only then will the Kingdoms of this world become the Kingdoms of our Lord and His Christ.

Eternal Blessings,
Cynthia Alvarez

Cynthia Alvarez

Chapter One
Who Are God's Apostles?

The most fascinating movement is currently underway concerning God's strategic implementation of his end time agenda that is impacting the world at an accelerated rate. What is this movement? This current movement is the bringing forth of God's true Apostles for the work of the last days. Many prophecies have yet to be realized by the Body of Christ simply because the Apostles have not been in place to lead the body into more advanced knowledge and more in depth understanding of the Kingdom of God, as the Apostles are at the forefront of the Kingdom when it comes to the Body of Christ grasping the truth of that realm. Without the ministry of the Apostles, the Body of Christ moves at a snail's pace as it relates to spiritual growth and Kingdom matters. Why? Because the true Apostles of God have surpassed the other members and officers in the Body of Christ when it comes to having a more extensive overall understanding of the Kingdom of God through experience, wisdom, revelation, and relationship. It does not mean they are loved more by the Lord or that they are better than any other member of the body. It simply means that the Lord has chosen, fashioned, established, and entrusted them with a greater measure of His Kingdom holdings in the earth.

5

"And Jesus answered and said unto him, Blessed art thou, Simon Barjona: for flesh and blood hath not revealed it unto thee, but my Father which is in heaven. And I say also unto thee, that thou art Peter, and upon this rock I will build my church; and the gates of hell shall not prevail against it. And I will give unto thee the keys of the kingdom of heaven: and whatsoever thou shalt bind on earth shall be bound in heaven: and whatsoever thou shalt loose on earth shall be loosed in heaven." (Matthew 16:17-19)

Their responsibility is weightier and more complex than the average believer or officer in the Body of Christ because the rock that God's church is built upon happens to be the revelation of Jesus Christ and the truth of His Kingdom that has been revealed explicitly by the Father. And not only is the church built upon such revelation, but it is also sustained through continuous revelation that is released from the Lord Jesus Christ to the Apostles. Then that revelation is filtered down from the Apostles to the Body of Christ, so that a greater depth of the Kingdom of God can be realized on a corporate level. When this happens, the Body of Christ can experience a surge of movement, since answers and direction flow from revelation. The only other member or officer in the Body of Christ that can come close to understanding the work or mandate of an Apostle is the Prophet of God. Prophets have an impressive scope of knowledge concerning the Kingdom because they must work in partnership, so to speak with God's

Apostles. How do they work in partnership? They both work as a team to bring the Body of Christ into a more explicit understanding of the Kingdom of God, as well as into a more powerful and immediate reality of the Kingdom.

There is one thing that I want to make clear to everyone's understanding before I proceed any further. There is no such thing as a self-made Apostle, since Apostles are formed in the womb and groomed by the Lord himself throughout the course of their lives. It is Jesus Christ alone who fashions them for official service in the Kingdom of God. Too often erroneous teaching runs rampant in the Body of Christ, which leads to title chasing instead of believers maturing into their predestined place in God. Through erroneous teaching, many Christians are led to believe that they can fit into any role of choice within the Body of Christ, if they are taught how to do something. But this is not in agreement with the reality of the Kingdom of God.

"And God wrought special miracles by the hands of Paul: So that from his body were brought unto the sick handkerchiefs or aprons, and the diseases departed from them, and the evil spirits went out of them. "Then certain of the vagabond Jews, exorcists, took upon them to call over them which had evil spirits the name of the Lord Jesus, saying, we adjure you by Jesus whom Paul preaches. And there were seven sons of one Sceva, a Jew, and chief of the priests, which did so. And the evil spirit answered and said,

7

Jesus I know, and Paul I know; but who are ye? And the man in whom the evil spirit was leaped on them, and overcame them, and prevailed against them, so that they fled out of that house naked and wounded." (Acts 19:11-16)

Apostles are born to be Apostles because there are certain aspects or traits of their anointing that must come from their biological gene pool. Some aspects or traits of their anointing must come through training and other aspects must be imparted by the Spirit of God. He already knew every person who would be an Apostle before they were ever formed in the womb, which is why Apostle Paul goes into detail to make this truth known to us.

"For whom he did foreknow, he also did predestinate to be conformed to the image of his Son, that he might be the firstborn among many brethren. Moreover, whom he did predestinate, them he also called: and whom he called, them he also justified: and whom he justified, them he also glorified." (Romans 8:29-30)

In fact, everything pertaining to the inception and conception of an Apostle must be in complete agreement with God's prerequisites for that office, as the office of Apostle originates in heaven. Therefore, it is of the utmost importance for the precise genes, traits, and impartations to be inherent aspects of the foundation of the Apostle's nature, character and anointing. Jesus is the Chief Apostle from heaven. He is the first Apostle sent forth from the Father in heaven and everything pertaining to his inception and conception into the earth was carried out with the greatest detail. His biological gene pool was a necessary component for the foundation of his nature, character and anointing, which is why we see emphasis placed on his biological gene pool in the Gospel of Matthew Chapter One.

"The book of the generation of Jesus Christ, the son of David, the son of Abraham. Abraham begat Isaac; and Isaac begat Jacob; and Jacob begat Judas and his brethren; And Judas begat Phares and Zara of Thamar; and Phares begat Esrom; and Esrom begat Aram; And Aram begat Aminadab; and Aminadab begat Naasson; and Naasson begat Salmon; And Salmon begat Booz of Rachab; and Booz begat Obed of Ruth; and Obed begat Jesse; And Jesse begat David the king; and David the king begat Solomon of her that had been the wife *of Urias; And Solomon begat Roboam; and Roboam begat Abia; and Abia begat Asa; And Asa begat Josaphat; and Josaphat begat Joram; and Joram begat Ozias; And Ozias begat Joatham; and Joatham begat Achaz; and Achaz begat Ezekias; And Ezekias begat Manasses; and Manasses begat Amon; and Amon begat Josias; And Josias begat Jechonias and his brethren, about the time they were carried away to Babylon: And after they were brought to Babylon, Jechonias begat Salathiel; and*

Salathiel begat Zorobabel; And Zorobabel begat Abiud; and Abiud begat Eliakim; and Eliakim begat Azor; And Azor begat Sadoc; and Sadoc begat Achim; and Achim begat Eliud; And Eliud begat Eleazar; and Eleazar begat Matthan; and Matthan begat Jacob; And Jacob begat Joseph the husband of Mary, of whom was born Jesus, who is called Christ. So, all the generations from Abraham to David are fourteen generations; and from David until the carrying away into Babylon are fourteen generations; and from the carrying away into Babylon unto Christ are fourteen generations." (Matthew 1:1-17)

The Gospel of Matthew begins with a tour of his biological genealogy to further build on the fact that the gene pool is an essential component of an Apostle's anointing. Even so, there are aspects of the anointing that can only be realized through training and development but are no less important than the biological gene pool traits, as there is not one Apostle who can function wholly without these attributes. Some examples of such qualities and traits would be determination, endurance, diligence and resilience. These are not qualities that he is born with, but they are traits that are gained over the course of his lifetime through intense training simulations, which are better known as fiery trials. If these notable traits are missing from the compounded nature of an Apostle, he will not be capable of operating at his fullest potential. It would be impossible for an Apostle to operate sufficiently without the traits of his biological gene pool and qualities gained through training. In fact, it would be utterly foolish to ever think he could function from the divine spiritual realm without being enhanced or upgraded with supernatural qualities from the Spirit of God. The power of God would not be accessible to him, nor could the authority of that office be a reality for him. It simply cannot happen. So, to consider that someone can become an Apostle just because they choose to pursue the path of an Apostle and be trained as one is erroneous and far-fetched. An Apostle is not authenticated by a title, but by a complex mixture of innate qualities, imparted substance, and defined traits that constitute his distinctive anointing. It is important to understand that every person of the Godhead is involved in the blending of this specific anointing. If the entire Godhead is not involved, how can Apostles have the Lord's angelic host or fleet at their disposal, that Jesus is involved? How can Apostles have access to the Throne Room of God, except that the Father is involved? How else can Apostles perform miracles and wonders, except that the Spirit of God is involved? So, we see that the Spirit of God dispenses the gifts to the individual, while the Lord Jesus decides which gifts the individual receives and how the gifts are compounded to formulate an anointing that is unique to an Apostle. Then the Father God decides in what capacity the Apostle will function. For example: One individual might be ordained to be an Apostle to a local community or city. Another might be ordained on a broader level for a national ministry, and others ordained for an international role. It is the Father's will in any case, as he has predestined them to be such ministers of the Gospel of the Kingdom.

"Now there are diversities of gifts, but the same Spirit. And there are differences of administrations, but the same Lord. And there are diversities of operations, but it is the same God which worketh all in all." (I Corinthians 12:4-5)

Because Apostles are born and not self-made, there is a need for them to be groomed and conditioned for the office they have been appointed to. In other words, they must go through a rigorous developing and conditioning process that many in the Body of Christ will never experience simply because they have no need to endure that level of processing. In fact, many believers would not be able to endure such a gruesome, arduous, and extreme process as that of an Apostle. The process must be implemented in such an extreme and strenuous manner, since the nature of the mandate, power and authority attached to the office of an Apostle is interwoven in God's sovereignty. The office cannot be separated from God, nor can God be separated from it because the office itself is an extension of God and bears his power and executes his will. And whoever is placed in the office must become the very expression of God in nature, power, and in authority. So, we see that everyone is not suitable for the office of Apostle, nor is the office of Apostle suitable for everyone.

When God's appointed time arrives for a person to begin the journey towards the office of Apostle, the individual does not immediately know that they are to be an Apostle. Why? Because the first part of the process of an Apostle is to be broken by the sovereign hand of God. It is a process that is designed to bring death to the flesh-nature or self-nature, which is the purpose of the extremely unusual fiery trials, struggles, and persecutions that every destined Apostle must endure. He must be broken in every area of his life by the hand of God to separate or detach him from all ties to world systems, traditions, and cultures that have influenced the very core of his being up to this point in time. God must bring the person to the end of their own self-sufficiency. The end of their way of thinking. The end of how they feel about everything. The end of their will being in total control of every aspect of their life. God must use the process as an intervention to put that filthy, rebellious, and sinful flesh nature to death, so that he can begin to fashion the person into the image he has predestined them to become. Please understand that the breaking process for such a person is not short-lived when compared to other members in the Body of Christ. But it is an extremely lengthy process that spans across years, even decades because it takes an undetermined measure of time for the flesh-nature to be overcome and total detoxification from the world systems to take place for one who is predestined to the office of Apostle. It is not a cake walk as some might imagine it to be, but it is an utter death walk. The flesh-nature must be put to death with every step that is taken while leaving no option whatsoever for compromise. Now, I know many Christians will claim that their individual processes have been just as intense as an Apostle's process, so they do not see why greater emphasis is being placed on one and not the other's process. Well, it is not about placing more emphasis on one person over another to belittle anyone. It is about understanding who God's Apostles are and grasping the truth of their purpose in Him. Without perceiving the significance of their process, it would be difficult for anyone to grasp even the tiniest revelation about Apostles. To help your understanding of the reasoning behind the difference in the process of Apostles in comparison to other members in the Body of Christ, I will tell you plainly that Apostles must spiritually enter and possess the Kingdom of God ahead of the rest of the Body of Christ, which is why they seem to surpass or transcend everyone else in spiritual development. The nature and mantle of the office requires acceleration in the Spirit for them, since the office itself proceeds forth from heaven to earth and not from earth to heaven. So, we can begin to clearly see that the entire life and ministry of Apostles is centered around the Kingdom of God because every servant, minister, and clergyman must minister from their spiritual level. In doing so, they each are empowered and indebted to speak of that which they have seen, heard, and experienced spiritually.

"And when I saw him, I fell at his feet as dead. And he laid his right hand upon me, saying unto me, Fear not; I am the first and the last: I am *he that liveth, and was dead; and, behold, I am alive for evermore, amen; and have the keys of hell and of death. Write the things which thou hast seen, and the things which are, and the things which shall be hereafter;" (Revelation 1:17-19)*

Having surpassed others in entering and possessing the Kingdom, the complete orientation of Apostles is Kingdom, Kingdom, and more Kingdom! I will be expounding further on this matter in upcoming chapters, but keep in mind that Apostles are commissioned from the Kingdom and positioned in the Kingdom simultaneously; therefore, their stance will never change nor will their mission be abated.

Cynthia Alvarez

Chapter Two
Why Do We Need Apostles?

Now that the previous chapter has somewhat familiarized you with God's true Apostles, let's talk about why we need Apostles in the world today. I know someone already thinks that they will be just fine with or without the ministry of an Apostle in their life. Well, if you are reading this book and feel that you do not need an Apostle one way or the other, I'm here to tell you plainly that your life is stuck in a pit with no way out. You cannot see your destiny because you do not know your destiny without the ministry of an Apostle. You think you are okay and on the move for God, but you have simply been circling the same mountain, which is what stuck folk do. They are unable to make any notable progress towards spiritual growth or Kingdom possession since they are limited to the same mediocre experience day in and day out. If the truth would be told, it is a frustrating and powerless state to be confined to, as there is no glory in being stuck and falling short of destiny. In fact, there is only shame, regret, and gnashing of teeth for such misfortune. But guiding you safely to your destined place is only a portion of the ministry work of Apostles. Whether many people know it or not, the bulk of an Apostle's work involves spiritual warfare.

"For we wrestle not against flesh and blood, but against principalities, against powers, against the rulers of the darkness of this world, against spiritual wickedness in high places." (Ephesians 6:12)

Although the language of an Apostle is always Kingdom oriented, it is also a language interwoven in combat and aggression. So, if you engage in conversation with this officer of God, prepare to hear more extensive insight about the Kingdom of God, more potent warfare strategies, encounters of direct face-offs with demonic principalities, insight concerning wickedness in high places, interaction and joint ventures with God's angelic army, as well as countless experiences that take place in the Throne Room of God. Prepare to hear magnificent and unbelievable things that you have not been privy to until now because an Apostle is continually revealing the mysteries of the Kingdom of God to bring the Body of Christ into closer proximity and a much richer reality of the Lord's realm. The bible is replete with Apostolic revelation that gives us glimpses of different aspects of God's heavenly realm.

Glimpses of the Kingdom of God through Apostolic Revelation:

Jesus reveals that believers have physical homes in the Kingdom of God.

"Let not your heart be troubled; ye believe in God, believe also in me. In my Father's house are many mansions: if it were not

18

so I would have told you. I go to prepare a place for you. And if I go and prepare a place for you, I will come again, and receive you unto myself; that where I am, there ye may be also." (John 14:1-3)

Paul reveals the reality of Heaven.

"And I knew such a man, (whether in the body, or out the body, I cannot tell: God knoweth;) How that he was caught up into paradise, and heard unspeakable words, which it is not lawful for a man to utter." (II Corinthians 12:1)

John reveals details of the Throne Room of God.

"And immediately I was in the spirit: and, behold, a throne was set in heaven, and one sat on the throne. And he that sat was to look upon like a jasper and a sardine stone: and there was a rainbow round about the throne, in sight like unto an emerald. And round about the throne were four and twenty seats: and upon the seats I saw four and twenty elders sitting, clothed in white raiment; and they had on their head crowns of gold. And out the throne proceeded lightnings and thundering and voices; and there were seven lamps of fire burning before the throne, which are the seven Spirits of God. And before the throne there was a sea of glass like unto crystal; and in the midst of the throne, and round about the throne, were four beasts full of eyes before and behind." (Revelations 4:2-6)

For the average believer, it is something wonderful to look forward to, but for this officer of the Kingdom, it is already a reality. They speak that which they know through first-hand experience, divine revelation, and what is received as frontline directives from God. It is no wonder this officer has a Kingdom orientation or outlook in all matters. He literally belongs to another world or realm. In other words, he exists in this world with the purpose of bringing the Body of Christ into God's realm. We must have a firm understanding that Apostles have been taken from among men and cut-off from the systems of this world by the will of God in every area of their lives, so that they can be properly groomed by him for the full scope work of Kingdom Ambassadors. Don't misunderstand me, they have extensive knowledge and experience in the systems of this world, as God does not take them out of the world systems until they have indeed been exposed to all that he deems is necessary for the ministry of this officer. Since they have been taken out and groomed in such a manner for such a work, we know that at an appointed time, God will send his Apostles back to the world that they once left to accomplish his will and spearhead his movements.

"Ye have not chosen me, but I have chosen you, and ordained you, that ye should go and bring forth fruit, and that your fruit should remain; that whatsoever ye shall ask of the Father in my name, he may give it you." (John 15:16)

If we are to perceive, grasp, and move into the truth of many prophecies that were spoken ages ago and are to be fulfilled in this present generation, we will need the work of the Apostles to be able to do so. If we are to understand our individual and collective roles in this hour, we will need the work of the Apostles to be able to do so. If we are to see the Body of Christ advancing towards the appointed Kingdom Age in hopes of fulfilling the high call of God in Christ Jesus, we will need the work of the Apostles to be able to do so. It is the Apostles who understand how to piece together revelation and prophecy to reveal the big picture that would otherwise be difficult for others to grasp.

Cynthia Alvarez

Chapter Three
The Realm of the Apostles

In Chapter Two, we discussed the importance of Apostles being on the scene in today's world and learned that if these powerful Kingdom officials do not appear in ruling spheres of this world, believers will never rise to the stature of dominion. In other words, the Body of Christ will never be qualified to rule and reign as heirs and joint-heirs with Christ. Nor will the Kingdom of God be physically revealed in the earthly realm, since the Apostles' work is to establish the Kingdom of God on planet earth. So, it is necessary that we shift our focus to understanding the realm of the Apostles of God. If we can comprehend the realm that they abide in and operate from, we can breakthrough many traditional strongholds that have been so successful in locking believers into an underdeveloped mental capacity concerning the Kingdom of God. It is the responsibility of the Apostles to free believers from this captivity and liberate them into more expansive knowledge of the King and His Kingdom, which is not an easy task in and of itself. In working to liberate the Body of Christ from this place of captivity, Apostles must come against demonic strongholds, traditional strongholds, and the firm grip of ignorance because people who lack clear understanding of the King and His Kingdom

23

will fall prey to any belief system and doctrine that keep them in comfortable and familiar surroundings, which is much of what we see today. Yet, these are the same strongholds that God has delivered his mighty Apostles from, so that he can bring them into his divine realm.

"For the weapons of our warfare are not carnal, but mighty through God to the pulling down of strongholds; Casting down imaginations, and every high thing that exalts itself against the knowledge of God and bringing into captivity every thought to the obedience of Christ."   (II Corinthians 10:4-5)

Why does God bring them into his realm? He brings them into his realm for several reasons. First, Apostles are brought into the divine realm to see the excellency of His Kingdom and to be made fully aware of the degenerate state of the earthly realm. Secondly, Apostles are brought into the divine realm to give them a sure or solid testimony of the King and His Kingdom.

"And this voice came from heaven we heard, when we were with him in the holy mount. We have also a more sure word of prophecy; whereunto ye do well that ye take heed, as unto a light that shineth in a dark place, until the day dawn, and the day star arise in your hearts."   (II Peter 1:18-19)

Thirdly, Apostles are brought into the divine realm to grasp a comprehensive or more in depth understanding of the purpose and destiny of the Body of Christ. Lastly, Apostles are brought into the divine realm to understand the full scope of their Kingdom assignments or role.

By now, it should be clear that the realm of the Apostles is the Kingdom of God. Although they carry out their assignments in this earthly realm for the Lord God, these mighty officers comprehend quite well that their life and citizenship is in his realm. The numerous encounters they have with the Lord Jesus Christ and the extensiveness of their access into his realm further validates the sphere of their existence. How do they live in the realm of God when they are physically located in the earth? Apostles live there spiritually in this present time. Meaning that they have the capacity to live in the realm of God from a **mental perspective,** through **emotional stability**, and a **subjugated will,** as these areas of their lives must be at a level of maturity that is necessary to bring them into full alignment with God and allows them to abode in heavenly places while living in the physical realm. All areas that need daily regeneration in the lives of believers are areas that the Apostles have surpassed the rest of the Body of Christ in through maturation, which is why these officers are able to edify, build, and mature believers in Christ. By reason of the calling alone, Apostles are developed, pruned, and groomed by the Lord Jesus Christ to be qualified as leading officers in the Kingdom. So yes, they must be mentally developed, emotionally stable, and willfully engaged or engrossed in all things Kingdom.

Mental Perspective of Apostles

Apostles might currently reside in a physical body while in this earthly realm, but they spiritually abide in the heavenly realm of God. They are mentally aligned to his realm, so they have an accurate understanding of the things that are transpiring there. Apostles are experts at keeping their minds free of mental clutter and blockages that could interfere with God's spiritual flow in their lives, as their greatest need is to keep a clear and open line of communication with the Lord God.

"And be not conformed to this world; but be ye transformed by the renewing of your mind, that ye may prove what is that good, and acceptable, and perfect will of God." (Romans 12:2)

Furthermore, these officers never want anything to obstruct them from experiencing the heavenly visitations they have become accustomed to in the Spirit, since they certainly understand God has a specific spiritual network that he communicates through; linking or tapping into this network requires official access, which means that the entire Godhead is involved in the clearance or authorization that Apostles have to this network. I know someone wants to know why the entire Godhead is involved in the Apostles spiritual access to God's network when average believers have access to the spiritual network as well. Yes, believers have access to his network, but they do not have the same level of clearance that Apostles have, as the caliber of the assignment and nature of the duties of Apostles far outweigh that of average believers.

Apostles mental prowess in understanding their citizenship in heaven is unmatched by the rest of the Body of Christ. They are fluent in the details surrounding their position in Christ, as they have been briefed by the Lord many times over concerning their identity as a new creation in him. Therefore, they are well equipped in faith, skillful in assignment, and astute in spiritual matters. Without question, Apostles are mentally exceptional in the Spirit.

Emotional Stability of Apostles

The emotional stability of Apostles is astounding when considering the magnitude of the workload and obstacles they face as they forge ahead in establishing the Kingdom of God on earth. It is not easy to remain emotionally balanced when your life is always in peril, believers are constantly needing your support, struggles are too numerous to count, and the Kingdom of Darkness keeps you on their most wanted list year-round. Yet, these magnificent officers of the Lord are more than capable of keeping their flesh subdued and emotions in check. Apostles know exactly what it takes to make sure their emotions are stabilized and aligned with God's heart to ensure that feelings do not impede their purpose in Christ.

"And every man that strives for the mastery is temperate in all things. Now they do it to obtain a corruptible crown; but we and incorruptible. I therefore so run, not as uncertainly; so, fight I, not as one that beats the air: But I keep under my body, and bring it into subjection: lest that by any means, when I have preached to others, I myself should be a castaway." (I Corinthians 9:25-27)

Keeping our emotions aligned to God's will takes work. It does not happen overnight, and every genuine Apostle of the Lord understands this reality. Prayer, fasting, and intaking the word of God daily are proven stabilizers of the heart or seat of emotions. In many cases our emotions must be forced into alignment with God's will and heart. With our mind, we perceive his will, but it is with our heart that we accept or reject his will. For this reason, the condition of a person's heart is a serious matter to the Lord God. As a matter of fact, it is the heart of a person that steers their faith towards God to partake of his righteousness.

"For with the heart man believeth unto righteousness; and with the mouth confession is made unto salvation." (Romans 10:10)

So, if Apostles are to establish the Kingdom of God on earth, they must first establish it in the heart of men, which is easier said than done. Before people come into the knowledge of the Lord Jesus Christ, their hearts are dark and evil, as they have no truth and insight pertaining to God. They are lost in darkness until they receive light or truth that is only available in Christ. This light or truth is what Apostles establish in the hearts of men as they extend the Kingdom of God, since they understand that the durability or longevity of the Kingdom on earth is solidified when believers reach the level of emotional stability necessary to be unshakeable by the ever-changing circumstances of life.

"Therefore, my beloved brethren, be ye steadfast, unmovable, always abounding in the work of the Lord, forasmuch as ye know that your labor is not in vain in the Lord." (I Corinthians 15:58)

The ability to manage and subdue the inner seat of emotions or heart affords Apostles the benefit of experiencing the joy and eternal bliss of God's realm while executing their Kingdom assignment on earth.

The Will of Apostles

One of the most important things to know about Apostles is that the Lord's will is their will. They are implicitly submitted to his will, since Apostles are in essence bona fide officials of the Kingdom. Additionally, their seat or base of operation stems from his realm and can be seen in the fact that the Lord God grooms them for a higher sphere of occupancy and dominion. How are they groomed for a higher sphere? It can be seen in the overall extensive process that Apostles must endure at the behest of the Lord. Many extremely gruesome trials must be endured by these officers because their will must be brought into full submission to the sovereign will of the Lord God, so that they can function as the high caliber servants that the Lord requires them to be.

"Beloved, think it not strange concerning the fiery trial which is to try you, as though some strange thing happened unto you: But rejoice, inasmuch as ye are partakers of Christ's sufferings; that, when his glory shall be revealed, ye may be glad also with exceeding joy." (I Peter 4:12-13)

The gruesome trials they encounter promote discipline, involve training, and teaches them obedience, as the trials force their will out of commission until the only operative purpose remaining in their lives is the Lord's objective. In other words, Apostles are figuratively beaten into submission to prepare them for his service. I know it sounds harsh and seems wrong on many levels for Apostles to endure so much affliction, which ultimately causes them to relinquish the entirety of their will to the Lord. Yet, releasing their will allows them to become fully clothed in his will and brings them face to face with the sovereign God. This is the reason Apostles are staunch defenders of the Kingdom and faithful executors of his will. They experience the Lord up close and in a more personal way than the rest of the Body of Christ. It is impossible to encounter him at the level that these officers do and not be submitted to his will in every way. Please do not jump to the wrong conclusion by thinking that these officers are unhappy with this submissive nature and would much rather be able to mete out the course of their own lives. Apostles clearly understand they are in the best position possible by being submitted to him because they have access, authority, and interactions with the Lord God that the rest of the Body of Christ is not privy to. In fact, they consider being a servant of the Lord God to be the greatest honor and privilege that one can experience in this earthly realm, even if it has cost them everything.

Cynthia Alvarez

Chapter Four
What is Significant About
the Work of Apostles?

In the previous chapter we discussed the realm of the Apostles to shed light on the Kingdom orientation of these mighty officers. Understanding more about the orientation of Apostles allows us to better comprehend the significance of the scope of their work. The work or assignment of Apostles is more impressive and expansive than many believers even know. So often, Apostles are viewed as nothing more than church planters in the Kingdom of God. But this perspective presents a very shallow interpretation of the role or function of the chief officer of the Lord God. Again, the assignment is too expansive to be confined to the church only, as it is a work of Kingdom proportion. Apostles do more than just planting churches across the globe, they establish the Kingdom of God throughout the earth. If they are establishing the Kingdom, it means they are bringing order in the earth. Not only are they bringing order, but it is the sovereign and divine order or will of God that is being set in place. However, many people think the only place the Kingdom of God will ever be legitimately recognized or acknowledged is in a church building or religious edifice. Yet, the Kingdom of God is to encompass the entirety of the earth, which means when it is fully manifested, the Kingdom will have dominion in every sphere of authority or influence in this realm, as it must be realized as the preeminent global culture in the earth.

We must understand that the work of Apostles is a Kingdom assignment, which means that if the rest of the Body of Christ is to grasp this truth, they will need more detailed insight into this matter. For this reason, Apostles are always poised to deliver the 'Who', 'What', 'When', 'Where', 'Why', and 'How' answers pertaining to the King and His Kingdom. In other words, these chief officers must have the capacity to shift the lives of believers with the answers they are dispensing. Why are they able to shift the lives of others with their words and ministry? The ability to shift or transition the lives of others is made possible because of the Apostles own personal life **experiences**, their **revelatory** level, and constant **proceedings** with the Lord God. Yes, these undeniable facets make them the most well-rounded officers in the Kingdom. Please do not misinterpret what is being said here. They are the most well-rounded, not the most well-loved in the Kingdom. God loves all believers with the same love.

Life Experiences

Apostles are the most well-rounded officers in the Kingdom because God knows the encounters, obstacles, and conflicts that are essential for their proper development in Christ.

34

We clearly comprehend that growth comes from lessons learned and knowledge application, but for Apostles to have the answers that will enrich the Body of Christ, they must have extensive life experiences. Why? They must be able to relate to everything that believers encounter. Whether it is the good, bad, or ugly that believers face, Apostles must be able to meet them right where they are mentally, emotionally, and physically.

"To the weak became I as weak, that I might gain the weak: I am made all things to all men, that I might by all means save some." (I Corinthians 9:22)

In short, this chief officer of the Lord God must be able to shift or change lives with lessons they have learned over the course of their own lives. Sometimes, believers will mistake the foreknowledge of Apostles as being prophecy because these individuals are encountering a specific situation for the very first time. But for the Apostles, it is simply knowledge that they have pulled from the knowledge repository of their inner anointing. It is important to know that this inner knowledge repository has cost Apostles everything. They have endured the greatest losses, harshest disappointments, severest pain, most immense humiliation, warfare extremities, and compounded hardships for the sake of the Kingdom assignment or call that they must effectively execute in the earthly realm.

"Are they ministers of Christ? (I speak as a fool) I am more; in labors more abundant, in stripes above measure, in

prisons more frequent, in deaths oft. Of the Jews five times received I forty stripes save one. Thrice was I beaten with rods, once was I stoned, thrice I suffered shipwreck, a night and a day I have been in the deep: In journeyings often, in perils of waters, in perils of robbers, in perils by the heathen, in perils in the city, in perils in the wilderness, in perils in the sea, in perils among false brethren. In weariness and painfulness, in watching often, in hunger and thirst, in fasting often, in cold and nakedness. Beside those things that are without, that which cometh upon me daily, the care of all the churches." (II Corinthians 11:23-28

Revelatory Level

The ability of Apostles to shift or transition the Body of Christ individually or corporately is undeniable, since fresh and abundant revelation is a major facet of this officer's ministry. Revelation stimulates movement and promotes acceleration on any level, which is something Apostles know far too well. Whenever the Body of Christ becomes stagnate in their development, oftentimes it is because they lack the revelation or divine knowledge needed to thrust them forward. In fact, it is easy to identify believers who are connected to an apostolic ministry, as they are much further along in spiritual development than the average believer who has no connection to apostolic ministry. Why? Because through revelation, Apostles gain more advanced knowledge and understanding of the Kingdom of God, which allows them to bring believers into a fuller and more solid understanding of the Lord and his domain. When believers disregard the existence and importance of Apostles, they do it to their own detriment because without receiving revelation dispensed by this officer, destiny is literally out of reach. And such believers are unable to reach the maturity level for dominion in the Kingdom. They simply fall short of becoming ruling heirs of the Kingdom.

"My people are destroyed for lack of knowledge; because thou hast rejected knowledge, I will also reject thee, that thou shalt be no priest to me." (Hosea 4:6)

Revelation also helps usher believers along their journey of destiny in similitude to how a road map discloses unknown details, which lead travelers to specific locales that are part and parcel of reaching an anticipated place. I do not care how much people want to believe they can become fully mature and reach destiny with little to no revelation, it is impossible. Its like having a car and running out of gas less than halfway to your intended destination. It does not matter that you started out with a little fuel and the best intentions of completing the trip, you simply did not have what it takes to make it to the desired place, seeing that you fell short of reaching the goal. And you will not move another inch unless some good Samaritan or AAA Towing Service brings you fuel to get you moving again. Well, it is the same for believers who think they have what it takes to make it to destiny without needing revelation.

They quickly find out that unless apostolic revelation is flowing into their lives, movement becomes impeded.

Proceedings with The Lord

The one thing that sets the assignment or ministry of Apostles apart from other believers and officers is the peculiar dealings they have with the Lord Jesus Christ, which becomes a major factor in the successful execution of their duties. Apostles' interactions with the Lord vary in purpose and degree based on the specifics of any undertaking or movement they are spearheading. Believe it or not, these officers spend an extensive measure of time with the Lord in what can be considered as Kingdom board meetings. There are also many occasions with the Lord that are regarded as times of refreshing for Apostles. In the Kingdom board meetings, the officers receive vital information, discuss problem areas within the Body of Christ, receive instructions for Kingdom expansion on earth, obtain blueprints for each phase of God's unfolding agenda, etc. Although Apostles teach in such a manner that brings believers into a fuller understanding of the Kingdom, they must also be capable of shifting the individual, corporate, and universal Body of Christ in a moment's notice as the Lord deems necessary for reasons known only to him. Furthermore, because Apostles are elite warriors, strategic commanders, and chief officers of the armies of the Lord, they encounter immense and continual warfare that could easily overcome the average believers.

But there is no need to worry, since Apostles are firmly groomed to successfully endure gruesome and extensive combat. Yet, there are times that the Lord will call them to Himself, so they can rest from the weariness of battle and be refreshed in his presence. Quite often, during the resting and refreshing of Apostles, the Lord will enhance or upgrade them in various areas of their being, so they can perform at a higher capacity regarding their assignment or role. In doing so, the Lord ensures that his Apostles can effectively impact, shift, and transform the lives of all those whom they encounter. Having constant interactions or proceedings with the Lord gives these officers a more sure, solid, and potent word than the rest of the Body of Christ. For this reason, the work of Apostles spans far beyond the church world to reach the expanse of the Kingdom, since they are the chief Kingdom officers of the Lord. Because they are Kingdom officers, Apostles have an unchanging mission to transform this foreign earthly realm into an extension of God's Eternal and Sovereign Kingdom, which is why their interactions with the Lord are essential to the scope of their assignments.

The role of an Apostle is baffling when we take into consideration the more intricate details of their responsibilities. Did you know that Apostles carry the very seed of what they are assigned to establish? Yes, they carry within their spirit every seed of the Kingdom assignment that God has entrusted to them, which means they carry the seed for the blueprint of the ministry that they are sent to establish. They carry the seed of the fivefold officers who will be reared and groomed by them. They also carry the seed of destiny for every individual who will be birthed forth from their ministry. This is the reason Apostles have such a resilience about them, as they understand the weight of responsibility that is upon them. The seed of multitudes is within them. So, if God does not continue to reveal his Apostles in this era, the seeds within them cannot be sown into the lives of believers whom God has predestined to rise as heirs and joint-heirs with Christ. With so much riding on the work of these mighty officers, God must ensure they have the required leverage and support for such an enormous undertaking, which makes it obvious that the relationship between God and his Apostles is anything but ordinary. In fact, it is rather extraordinary by all accounts. We will take a closer look at this relationship in the following chapters. But the one thing I want to embed in the mind of everyone who reads this book, is that God will never plant anything in us that he is unable to harvest from us. In other words, God has placed the seeds of the Kingdom within his Apostles and at an appointed time, He is expecting a harvest of Kingdom proportion to come forth from these chief officers. Although they are appointed an immense level of work, it is stupefying to know that Apostles usually have little to nothing in the form of resources, finances, or manpower when it comes to the onset of executing their Kingdom assignment. No, they do not begin with a bed of roses and a great number of supporters. Instead, they must make things happen with what God has placed in them. They must use their spiritual expertise, standing Kingdom authority, spiritual affluence, and Christ endowed wisdom to establish or manifest the Kingdom of God in their assigned earthly jurisdictions. They must be capable of attracting a following with the message of the Kingdom that God has entrusted to them. Not only should they have a message, but they should be fully apt to demonstrate the powers of the Kingdom through deliverance, healing, and illuminating the hearts and minds of men. Once the message of the Kingdom is preached and received in faith by individuals, the powers of the Kingdom can be demonstrated by Apostles to impact the very core of their lives, thereby causing an extension of the Kingdom of God on earth. Once established, it continues to expand through the efforts of these mighty officers and those who have joined their undertakings.

Cynthia Alvarez

Chapter Five
The Authority and Power
Invested in Apostles

If there is anything that can captivate the minds of people and stop them right in their tracks, it would be the authority and power that Apostles operate in. There is nothing that compares to it on this side of heaven. You will never find a more powerful vessel of the Lord Jesus Christ than his Apostles. So, you might as well stop the toil of searching because you will not find any individual or officer who has been groomed, fashioned, and empowered to such a degree. These mighty officers have not been reared up and assigned to recover just a few people for the Lord Jesus Christ in this earthly realm. They have been brought into existence to recover Nations and Kingdoms for the Lord Jesus Christ. Yet, we must understand that it takes more than just reciting scriptures, holding a few church meetings, and passing out flyers inviting people to a church building when the Lord's express goal is that of recovering the Nations and Kingdoms of this world. Since such a task must target the spheres that influence the cultures of this world, it will take a more expanded degree of authority and a more upgraded level of power to accomplish *this endeavor for the Lord.*

43

"And the seventh angel sounded; and there were great voices in heaven, saying, the kingdoms of this world are become the kingdoms of our Lord, and of his Christ; and he shall reign forever and ever." (Revelation 11:15)

Apostles are empowered to recover the highest seats of authority in the influential spheres of culture, which is something that no other individuals or officers will be able to accomplish, since the roles of the various leaders and officers in the Body of Christ vary in accordance to his will. But make no mistake about it, his Apostles have the highest call or assignment concerning the recovery work of the Nations and Kingdoms in this hour. Jesus already accomplished the greatest work by defeating the god of this world (Satan) on the cross. Satan is the highest level of authority in the Kingdom of Darkness and he has already been defeated. So now, Apostles must overcome and displace wickedness in high places, which happens to be the powerful governing seats of authority over Nations and Kingdoms.

"Ask of me, and I will give thee the heathen for thine inheritance, and the uttermost parts of the earth for they possession." (Psalms 2:8)

This wickedness is seen in every sphere of cultural influence. It is seen in the spheres of **family**, **business**, **entertainment**, **media**, **education**, **government**, **and religion**. So, if Apostles are to be successful in the Kingdom work that has been delegated to them by the Lord Jesus Christ, they must displace the demonic influences that hold sway over the highest level of authority in these spheres.

Family

The cultural sphere of family has deteriorated to being anything other than the glorious institution God ordained it to be. Households are torn apart because husbands and wives are no longer walking together as one. Instead, they have separate agendas that pull them in different directions and keeps them at odds with one another. Children nowadays have access to much more knowledge and information through technology, as well as being more spiritually intuitive than any previous generation of the 20th and 21st centuries, as many are prophetically inclined with little to no understanding about it. Because they are prophetically inclined, they can be impacted by persons and things in the spiritual realm. Yet, they have no understanding of the prophetic or their aptitude in the prophetic, which leaves them as open prey for demonic scouts from the Kingdom of Darkness. It also causes them to be gravely oppressed mentally and emotionally by such spirits. This leads to behavior that reflects their mental and emotional states of oppression, which manifests in their defiance or resistance to authority. In fact, they feel that since they are indeed highly intuitive and possess a great deal of knowledge, there is no need to listen to or obey parents and other forms of governing authority, which has led to rebellion running rampant in households across the globe.

"There is a generation that curseth their father, and doth not bless their mother. There is a generation that are pure in their own eyes, and yet is not washed from their filthiness." (Proverbs 30:11)

Grandparents no longer desire to preserve and secure a godly foundation or heritage for future generations, as they are more concerned with preserving their youth and vitality in attempts to overcome old age. So, they do not have time to build, empower, and enrich the lives of those coming after them. They would much rather party, date, and appease their fleshly desires than to solidify their role as the patriarchs and matriarchs in the family lineage. Yet, it is wonderful to know that restoring family order and structure is an aspect within the mantle of Apostles. They have been given the power, responsibility, and jurisdiction necessary to reclaim the cultural sphere of family for the Lord Jesus Christ.

Business

The cultural sphere of business is spinning out of control, as it has surely become the habitation of the spiritual fowls of the air. Meaning that it has become an institution governed by wickedness and greed instead of being governed through integrity and righteousness. Businesses have allowed the lure of financial enrichment to outweigh the essential purpose of being institutions that provide services, which fulfill the needs of mankind. Yes, the purpose of business is to provide services that meet needs for mankind and to be reasonably recompensed for such provisions. Unfortunately, the need to rake in huge amounts of revenue by businesses has caused them to provide services through methods that take advantage of the less fortunate status of billions of people across the globe.

"But they that will be rich fall into temptation and a snare, and into many foolish and hurtful lusts, which drown men in destruction and perdition. For the love of money is the root of all evil; which while some coveted after, they have erred from the faith, and pierced themselves through with many sorrows." (I Timothy 6:9-10)

One only needs to look at the medical industry to see the immense scope of degradation in the cultural sphere of business. Many people across the globe have health issues that could be successfully managed through a healthier lifestyle of exercise and improved eating habits. Yet, many medical doctors would rather prescribe their patients medications that in most cases are required to be taken for the rest of their lives, while causing damage to other areas in the physical body. Prescribing medication is not only seen as a benefit for the patients, but it is also advantageous to the pharmaceutical industry. The more prescriptions doctors hand out to their patients, the more secure and stabilized the pharmaceutical industry becomes, as the number of patients needing prescriptions increase, the demand for medications catapults the pharmaceutical industry to a place of dominion. And along with the medical insurance companies who are also part and parcel of this medical monopoly that capitalizes on the essential and dire needs of society, greed itself flourishes and runs rampant. Yet, all hope is not lost, since the tapestry of the Apostles' mantle includes functionality in the marketplace or in businesses. As with the spheres of religion and family, they have been given the power, responsibility, and jurisdiction necessary to reclaim the cultural sphere of business for the Lord Jesus Christ.

Entertainment

For many believers in the Body of Christ and religious groups in the world, the cultural sphere of entertainment is one that they tend to avoid all together. Although they are fully aware of the degenerate condition of this influential sphere or realm, many would rather play it safe and have nothing to do with it on any level. But if it is one of the standing cultural spheres in the earth, we cannot leave it as is and think we can successfully recover all that belongs to the Lord. The earth is the Lord's and the fullness thereof, so that means whatever spheres of cultural influence exist, they belong to the Lord and all the increase that comes forth from them is his possession by default.

"The earth is the Lord's, and the fulness thereof; the world, and they that dwell therein."   (Psalms 24:1)

Furthermore, if we avoid tackling this mountain simply because of its present and past condition, we do the Lord a great injustice, since the global entertainment industry would be a great trophy prize for him. This sphere of culture involves arts, music, sports, theatrics, etc. It is one of the most prized possessions of the Kingdom of Darkness, since believers and religious groups are bent on evading any dealings with this sphere of culture. Yet, the Lord is not moved by man's presumptions, as he has equipped the Apostolic mantle for the recouping of this entertainment sphere. Please understand that he never harbors any bad feelings when believers or religious groups denounce any dealings with this sphere. The Lord does not expect them to attempt to engage in work that is beyond the scope of their specific mantles. It is the Apostles who must recover the ruling seat of authority in the cultural sphere of entertainment. Until that is done, no matter how much believers attempt to do a work in this sphere, it will not fall back into the hands of the Lord if the Apostles do not recover it. Once it is recovered by them, the rest of the Body of Christ can then move in and take the remaining seats of authority that exist within that sphere. Once again, as referenced to the previous three spheres, Apostles have been given the power, responsibility, and jurisdiction necessary to reclaim the cultural sphere of entertainment for the Lord Jesus Christ.

Media

It does not require a rocket scientist to understand the necessity of recovering the cultural sphere of media for the Lord. This is a powerful sphere that causes immediate change in the minds and hearts of man. In fact, it is by far the quickest and most effective method of establishing a movement of any nature. Technology makes it accessible for everyone and the plethora of outlets that exist today make it possible for anyone to have a platform from which they can push their own agenda. So, if there are over 7 billion people in the world who can be reached through these media outlets, the dynamics of their mindset can be impacted by just a few words being released on a platform in this sphere. That's right. People can become enraged, motivated, disappointed, disgruntled, excited, miserable, bias, and so on by what is released from the platforms of the media.

"Why do the heathen rage, and the people imagine a vain thing? The kings of the earth set themselves, and the rulers take counsel together against the Lord, and against his anointed." (Psalms 2:1-2)

Why would anyone think that the Lord is content with this cultural sphere remaining under the jurisdiction of the enemies of God? It is absurd to even consider that. The Lord is bringing his Apostles forth in this hour to initiate his movements, so it would only be befitting for them to recover this sphere and regain control of the media outlets to create platforms that will propel the Lord's agenda to the place of preeminence in all spheres of this realm. We already know they have been given power, responsibility, and jurisdiction necessary to reclaim the cultural sphere of media for the Lord.

Education

Education is an essential aspect of the cultures of this world. Without the cultural sphere of education being a factual aspect in this realm, we could not successfully function in any other sphere of cultural influence because we need to understand at least the fundamentals of operating in other spheres. Yet, learning and being molded to a culture requires the work of teachers or educators, which is the reason the Lord must recoup this specific sphere, since while it is under the sway of the enemy, the educators are given the right of way to teach on every subject in existence except teach about the King and His Kingdom. And if the King and the Kingdom are not being taught, society will not know the reason the Lord must reclaim this sphere of education because they will not possess the mental capacity to comprehend it. Yet, this is the reason that in most cases, he personally grooms and educates his Apostles on the backside of the desert, so to speak. He does not have time to wait for mankind to slowly and painfully make itty bitty baby steps before they can even understand the smallest truth concerning recovering this sphere. But he thoroughly grooms and equips Apostles for such an undertaking. They understand his purpose and their role in the scheme of all things to the letter. So, this is the reason we can confidently declare that Apostles' mantle includes functionality in every cultural sphere in this planet, as they have been given power, responsibility, and jurisdiction necessary to reclaim the cultural sphere of education for the Lord.

"Go ye therefore, and teach all nations, baptizing them in the name of the Father, and of the Son, and of the Holy Ghost: Teaching them to observe all things whatsoever I have commanded you: and lo, I am with you always, even unto the end of the world." (Matthew 28:19-20)

Government

The name of this sphere speaks for itself and speaks to the purpose of every believer, especially Apostles. Government is indictive of authority and power, so its clear that the cultural sphere of government must be placed back into the hands of the Lord Jesus Christ. He must have absolute control of every level of authority that exists in this earthly realm. There is no area of authority that will not become subject to his sovereignty, which means every nation, kingdom, and tribe will be his possession.

"For unto us a child is born, unto us a son is given: and the government shall be upon his shoulder: and his name shall be called Wonderful, Counsellor, The mighty God, The everlasting Father, The Prince of Peace. Of the increase of his government and peace there shall be no end, upon the throne of David, and

upon his kingdom, to order it, and to establish it with judgment and with justice from henceforth even forever. The zeal of the Lord of hosts will perform this." (Isaiah 9:6-7)

For far too long the nations of this world have used this cultural sphere to push agendas that excluded the Lord. The results of these agendas have been degrading and hostile to humanity on all scales. Wars are constantly at the forefront of the news, we are forced to recognize man instituted laws that make all manner of sin legal, governing officials have made lies and deception become the norm in society, sexual misconduct among governing officials is swept under the rug of the conscience of nations, morality has become an offense, while immorality has emerged as a sign of strength in this degenerate world. Yet, God is not moved by these atrocities whatsoever. He has already begun bringing his secret weapons (Apostles) to the forefront for such a time as this. These mighty officers are well able to take the cultural sphere of government and reaffirm it to the Lord Jesus Christ. All power belongs to him, no matter what nation, kingdom or tribe it is established in.

"And the seventh angel sounded; and there were great voices in heaven saying, the kingdoms of this world are become the kingdoms of our Lord, and of his Christ; and he shall reign forever and ever." (Revelation 11:15)

Yes, the Kingdoms or governments of this world will become the Kingdoms of our Lord and his Christ, as Apostles have

53

been given power, responsibility, and jurisdiction necessary to reclaim the cultural sphere of education for the Lord.

Religion

Believe it or not, religion has been a cultural sphere of great nuisance to the Lord Jesus Christ. He has watched from the heavenly realm as religion has been a miserable attempt of mankind to define his lordship and promote a genuine relationship with his person. And it does him no justice, since people who are drawn to religion instead of relationship never have an opportunity to know him intimately. Religion robs us of that opportunity. Instead of building and solidifying a relationship with the Lord, religion causes man to strive to know and adhere to traditions and ordinances of man, which in most cases excludes the Lord himself from being part of their pious activities.

"This people draweth nigh unto me with their mouth, and honoureth me with their lips; but their heart is far from me. But in vain do worship me, teaching for doctrines the commandments of men." (Matthew 15:8-9)

It's quite disheartening to know that such endeavors become nuisances to the Lord. Think about it for a moment. If you have a family that you love dearly who live out of state and you have gone through great lengths to make it possible for them to come visit you by purchasing the plane tickets, the hotel room and a rental car for them. They are eager to have this opportunity, not because they are excited to see you and spend time with you after being away from you for so long. But rather, they are excited about all that they can do because you provided everything for them. They are given the opportunity to take a trip with all expenses paid and are elated about the plans they have once they arrive at the place you want them to be. Yet, when they get in proximity to you, they decide to do everything that relates to what they consider important instead of spending time with you to enjoy intimate quality time that will build a more fortified relationship with you all. It's sad, but that is what happens when religion is hailed to higher importance than relationship with the Lord Jesus Christ. But no worries, God is intentional in his actions to recover this sphere of cultural influence. By now, we know with confidence that his Apostles have been given the power, responsibility, and jurisdiction necessary to reclaim the cultural sphere of religion for the Lord Jesus Christ.

Now that we see the magnitude of the workload Apostles have been assigned to, we understand the necessity of these officers being endowed with immense authority and power. In addition, we can also understand why many self-appointed Apostles, as well as other leaders within the Body of Christ who have attempted to take on the workload of the Lord's Apostles and have failed miserably. It is because these leaders are looking at the

Lord's Apostles after they have been installed into office. They are not viewing these mighty officers before they were installed as such. These onlookers who see the excellence of the Apostles in the execution of the Lord's will and the demonstration of the powers of the world to come, have no earthly idea of how these officers had to be brutally processed and fashioned by the hand of the Lord to become his chief officers in the Kingdom. So, when self-appointed Apostles and others think they can step into the role of these chief officers, we soon see them falling by the wayside, as they have not been built mentally, emotionally, or physically to carry out the mandate of his Apostles. They have not even considered the level of demonic warfare that the Kingdom of Darkness assigns to come against Apostles. But when these self-appointed Apostles encounter the fierce and continuous onslaughts of the enemies of God, they buckle under the weight of the assignment, the stress associated with it, and the demands of it. Some eventually walk away from the assignment all together, while others become so overwhelmed with the workload until their health begins to deteriorate, even to the point of death. Then there are those who are overpowered and brought into bondage by the enemy because they are not invested or endowed with the magnitude of authority and power the Lord gives to his Apostles. They are not equipped for such a role. It is no different than a mailman trying to handle the duties of a heart surgeon. Although the mailman thoroughly understands the duties assigned to him based on the position he is in, it does not mean that he is qualified to perform heart surgery. He knows nothing about the authority, duties, and skillset of a doctor. No, he knows nothing about what comes along with the territory of being a doctor, so he could certainly cause the death of a patient, if he is playing around in a hospital operating room without the necessary experience and knowledge in this field of work. He has no legal right to be in an operating room, just as a self-appointed Apostle has no legal right to the Kingdom office of Apostle, seeing that the Lord did not qualify him for such a mandate. Rest assured that the Lord sends his best equipped servants for the work of His Kingdom.

Cynthia Alvarez

Chapter Six
Apostles and Prophets
The Dream Team

In the previous chapter, we discussed the authority and power invested in God's Apostles as it relates to their Kingdom assignment or role. While they are in a class all by themselves, Apostles are also great Kingdom team players, especially when joining forces with Prophets. Although the work of both officers can be described as pivotal and powerful in every aspect, there is still nothing more awe inspiring than to see these two mighty offers working as a team to accomplish the will of God for His Kingdom on earth. As chief officers of the Lord, they are instrumental in breaking ground for the Kingdom, which means they are given the responsibility of impacting territories and lives that are resistant to the Lord and His Kingdom, as many people want nothing to do with Jesus or his government. Yet, these mighty officers not only break ground, but they are also the Kingdom's defense system. They spiritually shield or protect the Kingdom of God on earth in a similar manner as the ozone layer shields the natural inhabitants of earth from ultraviolet radiation. If the ozone layer is severely penetrated so that dangerous ultraviolet radiation successfully passes through this sphere or barrier of protection, many lives would be placed in harm's way because the atmosphere would become altered from its original state. When breached, the defense system is unable to safeguard the earth from imminent danger. In fact, the earth would be powerless against the effects of the ultraviolet rays that would invade it. Every creature on the planet would be susceptible to the effects of the radiation. Many people would be severely impacted on contact from the lethal rays while some would be moderately affected, if they took some measure of precaution by utilizing proper skincare treatments. Others who took evasive action in using proper skincare treatments and abiding in a place of shelter to avoid the ultraviolet rays would feel minimal effects of the radiation in their lives. In like manner, so it is with Apostles and Prophets. If intruders or contamination of any degree gains entrance into the Body of Christ, it would cause devastating effects in the Kingdom. Those who are weak in faith, would be severely impacted. Those who have some measure of validity in faith would be moderately affected while others who are stronger in faith would gradually become impacted by the breaches in the Kingdom. For this reason, these two chief officers must endure rigorous trials and encounter obstacles of unscaled magnitude to prepare them for the momentous work at hand. God must produce specific qualities within them to make them suitable Kingdom groundbreakers and certified defensive barriers. Without question, these officers must possess an extensive degree of **resolve, resilience,** and **reliability** if they are to properly safeguard the Kingdom. Nothing less will do, seeing that so much is at stake.

Resolve

No matter how intelligent, articulate, eager, popular or approachable any individual might be, if they do not possess the resolve that the Lord deems necessary to be a groundbreaker and defensive barrier for His Kingdom, he will never remotely consider them as possible candidates for either of these offices. Resolve is a non-negotiable qualification that Apostles and Prophets must possess, since they endure recurring high-level demonic assaults, setbacks, losses, disappointments, and betrayals.

"And Jesus said unto him, no man, having put his hand to the plough, and looking back, is fit for the kingdom of God." (Luke 9:62)

Without having a substantial measure of resolve, an individual would be ineffective in fulfilling the duties of God's officials. It would be impossible for them to withstand the strength of the adversaries of the Kingdom because their commitment to God and their official post would become easily compromised, as they would not be willing to endure the stress, brutality, and eventualities of such demanding offices. Unfortunately, resolve is something that simply cannot be overlooked when it comes to God appointing his officials.

Resilience

Apostles and Prophets are officers of the highest caliber in the Kingdom. They have a valuable Kingdom outlook that is central to the execution of their overall duties. For them, the King and His Kingdom are first and foremost in their lives, in fact, it is what fuels their passionate drive to see that the Kingdom is manifested on earth, even if it costs their lives. Having such an inner driving force enables them to bounce back or recover quickly from traumatic events in their lives that would easily take out the average believer. Whether it is physical illness, death of a loved one, loss of a job, or ostracization, these officers are not shaken to the point of abandoning their office. They continue to perform as proficiently as God requires of them.

"Yea doubtless, and I count all things but loss for the excellency of the knowledge of Christ Jesus my Lord: for whom I have suffered the loss of all things, and do count them but dung, that I may win Christ." (Philippian 3:8)

It is resilience that allows Apostles and Prophets to rise above adversity and continue to move forward in the Kingdom agenda of God. Without having the grit or resilience to make a quick comeback from any challenge or difficulty, the Kingdom would undoubtedly be overrun by the enemy. But God has appointed these mighty officers to break ground for the King and stand in the defense of the Kingdom to ensure that it is established and expanding according to his agenda. God does not make exceptions or retract his qualifications for these two officers. His standards are irrevocable concerning these Kingdom officials and he will not budge in the slightest detail, since the Kingdom is the overall subject at hand.

Reliability

Nothing is more pressing to God concerning Apostles and Prophets than their reliability. The extensive knowledge, dynamic gifts, and unfathomable revelations that have been entrusted to them by God means little to nothing, if he cannot depend on them being at his disposal.

"And when they had brought their ships to land, they forsook all, and followed him." (Luke 5:11)

So, to ensure that these officers always remain loyal to him, God will deal decisively and specifically with everything and everyone that has a tight grip on the heart of the Apostles and Prophets. Some of the relationships and connections to these officers will be terminated all together while other relationships will be revamped to fit within the specified guidelines that he has established in the lives of His Kingdom officers. Seeing that they spend most of their time in fellowship with God, it is only befitting that he takes great concern with who and what is connected to them. Why would he establish such powerful Kingdom offices, appoint chosen vessels to execute the duties of the offices, and send them forth into a foreign land that we know as this present evil world, yet not be concerned with them being reliable officials? Reliability is of the utmost importance, since they have been heavily endowed with his authority and power. As God continues to raise up Apostles and Prophets for the work of establishing His Kingdom, reliability will always be an interwoven thread in these mantles.

A unique and impressive quality of Apostles and Prophets is their ability to war effectively in the Spirit through decrees and fervent prayers. God has groomed these mighty officers to be fearless in the Spirit and a force to be reckoned with in battle. This can be clearly seen when they speak forth powerful decrees and amplified prayers, since these officers have phenomenal leverage in the spiritual realm and understand how to reach or hit the correct level or frequency needed to summon the angelic brigades of God. I know some people might not feel that it is a big deal that these officers can summon angelic assistance when necessary. But they do more than just speak forth a whisper to summon these angels. Apostles and Prophets speak with Kingdom authority and fervency because they summon angels from different levels and various spheres of the spiritual realm. So, it takes a specific pitch, special frequency, and certain grade of authority to cause God's mighty angelic army to heed the charge of men. Soft and timid spoken decrees will not muster the angelic forces needed to engage an army of darkness because it cannot yield the appropriate pitch or emit the proper signal needed to arouse God's celestial warriors. Nor will lukewarm and apathetic prayer bring about change on any level (spiritual or physical). Again, there is a certain pitch and frequency needed. In fact, with prayer, there is a certain temperature required. Prayer needs to reach a boiling point because it must ascend to a higher realm. It is no different than when water boils and turns into vapor. Only when the water vaporizes or transforms into a different form does it move higher into the atmosphere. Prayer is not meant to remain in the lower depths of the physical realm. But it is meant to ascend to the spiritual realm and impact that sphere to cause metamorphosis to take place in the earthly realm. Yes, decrees and prayers released from the mouths of Apostles and Prophets of God become weapons of mass destruction and mighty tools of Kingdom advancement. It stands to reason that he has meticulously crafted the anointing necessary to enable these two officers to strategically and fearlessly stand in gate of two realms and brandish immense power and authority to establish the Kingdom of God on earth.

"The effectual fervent prayer of a righteous man availeth much. Elias was a man subject to like passions as we are, and he prayed earnestly that it might not rain: and it rained not on the earth by the space of three years and six months. And he prayed again, and the heaven gave rain, and the earth brought forth her fruit." (James 5:16-18)

There is no questioning the weight of the workload of God's officers in this hour. Many people might see them as stringent and intransigent, as they refuse to deviate from the all-encompassing will of God. Apostles and Prophets are well versed in what they have been called to do for God. They are not ignorant to the impact they have on the Body of Christ, since much of what they do is geared towards keeping believers connected to the Person of God and not just making sure they are acquainted with his power. It is not enough that believers experience the power of God only, but they must form a genuine and intimate relationship with him to have dominion in the Kingdom. So, these officers lead believers into dominion by helping them forge a solid relationship with God above all else. Knowing that Satan is relentless in opposing or counteracting the formation of such a relationship between believers and God, these officers must remain staunch and stringent in the work of the Kingdom. If they falter at all in establishing believers in Christ and safeguarding the Kingdom, dominion would be beyond the scope of achievement for believers. Yet, the strength of Apostles and Prophets lies within their private and personal relationship with God. There is nothing quite like the bond between God and his chief officials. This relationship situates them as family, friends, and employees of the Almighty God; therefore, they encounter a broader scope of interactions with him that go far beyond what most believers experience. All believers are included in God's family or household because they are in Christ, but all believers are not considered to be his closest friends, as this level of relationship demands more from them. Being in friendship with God means that believers must grow in his knowledge and grace, since being friends means you both share interests and goals of some sort.

"Henceforth I call you not servants; for the servant knoweth not what his lord doeth: but I have called you friends; for all things that I have heard of my Father I have made known unto you." (John 15:14-15)

Yet, many believers show very little growth in his knowledge and grace, which means they simply cannot interact with his on a level of genuine friendship. However, being employed by God means that you are not only considered to be his family and friends, but you are trustworthy enough to handle Kingdom administration.

It is understood that for believers, God is the fullness of everything they will ever need. He is Lord, Savior, King, Father, Lawyer, Doctor, Provider, Protector, and much more because he has the credentials to support these claims. Furthermore, he also grooms his officers to be a fully functioning support system to effectively undergird the workload and meet the needs of the Body of Christ.

"To the weak became I as weak, that I might gain the weak: I am made all things to all men, that I might by all means save some. And this I do for the gospel's sake, that I might be partaker thereof with you." (I Corinthians 9:22-23)

So, when speaking of Apostles and Prophets, it becomes clear that God regards them as useful and beneficial to Kingdom administration. This is not to insinuate that they are loved by God more than any other believer, since God loves all believers with the same love. It is simply to give readers and idea of certain aspects of the work performed by these officers while keeping in mind that God chooses his officials and he will always do what is in the best interest of the Kingdom.

Chapter Seven
The Relationship Between Jesus and His Apostles

There is nothing more unique in its nature and of its kind than the relationship between the Lord Jesus Christ and His Apostles. The fact that the office of Apostle is not a product of the Church, but the Church is a product that stems from the mantle of the Apostle speaks volumes to our understanding. It is important that believers comprehend that the mantle or the responsibility of His Apostles does not start and stop with the Church. Their work is a Kingdom vocation from the start, as it reaches out to all spheres of authority or influence in the earthly realm. Since the role of these mighty officers is of global proportions, the Lord Jesus Christ would have to share the extent of his plans and authority with them.

"And he turned him unto his disciples, and said privately, Blessed are the eyes which see the things that ye see: For I tell you, that many prophets and kings have desired to see those things which ye see, and have not seen them; and to hear those things which ye hear, and have not heard them." (Luke 10:23-24)

I know someone is wondering why he shares so much with Apostles, seeing that he is the sovereign and omniscient God? Being omniscient is how he can predestine these officers before they are ever born into this world. Knowing the nature and caliber of such officers in advance, why would it be surprising to anyone that his relationship with them would be by far the most exceptional of all his officers? He entrusts them with greater authority, more extensive responsibilities, and a higher intimacy level with him. When Apostles reach the fullness of their calling or become mature in their walk as an Apostle, they become more than just servants to the Lord, they become his friends. They not only have an affiliation with him, but they have all things in common with the Lord Jesus Christ.

The relationship between the Lord and His Apostles is fascinating on all counts, as they share many concerns and characteristics that not only hints at their heightened level of intimacy, but it solidifies the sovereignty of their work. They both share the same Kingdom outlook. They both have had to utterly forsake their lives for the sake of establishing the Kingdom of God on earth. They both share a zero tolerance for sin and an all-encompassing love for righteousness. They both have the same perspective on what the Body of Christ should be. They are both masterful in combat or warfare and are multifaceted to say the least. The list goes on and on concerning the firmness of their relationship. In fact, the Lord himself sees to it that of all his officers, the Apostles are most compatible with his person and his will. Why? Because these are the mighty officers whom he entrusts with establishing His Kingdom in its fullness. So, this means that

Apostles are responsible for laying the proper foundation by imparting the rich eternal heritage of the Lord Jesus Christ in the hearts of men.

"According to the grace of God which is given unto me, as a wise master builder, I have laid the foundation, and another buildeth thereon. But let every man take heed how he buildeth thereupon. For other foundation can no man lay than that is laid, which is Jesus Christ." (I Corinthians 3:10-11)

Then they are to build the walls or establish the strength of the Kingdom through prophetic operation, which is why the place of Prophets is always considered to be on the walls of the Kingdom. After securing the walls, there is a need to fortify or ungird the Kingdom with pillars that support its purpose such as intercessors and stewards of Kingdom wealth. Next, expansion is necessary to effectively increase Kingdom influence in the earth, which means evangelizing must become highly operative in this undertaking. Once Kingdom expansion becomes a reality in the lives of believers, they must be shepherded or pastored to protect the Body of Christ or body of believers who are the Lord's most valuable assets from spiritual predators. Finally, the Kingdom must continue to be empowered and enlightened with knowledge, truth, and understanding that is imparted through teaching. Without each of these aspects being recognized as vital components in the establishing of the Kingdom of God, the purpose of the Lord would not be achieved. Yet, the strength and intimacy of the relationship between the Lord and His Apostles brings assurance that his purpose will always be established. In fact, the Lord is so confident in his mighty Apostles' faithfulness and obedience in establishing the Kingdom, that he has given them the keys (authority and power) of the Kingdom. In other words, the Lord Jesus Christ has invested within these officers everything they will ever need to manifest the fullness of His Kingdom on earth. If we were to look closer at what is mentioned concerning the various aspects of establishing the Kingdom, we would clearly see that the magnitude of the Apostles' mantle allows them to extend and institute other governing offices within the scope of their Kingdom assignment. Such offices are widely known as the fivefold offices (Apostle, Prophet, Evangelist, Pastor, and Teacher), which are essential components in edifying the Body of Christ. Because Apostles establish other governing offices, they have the capacity to properly define the role or duties pertaining to these seats of authority. Apostles know precisely what it takes to ensure the perpetuality of the Kingdom in the earth realm.

When we view the massive weight of responsibility that has been handed to Apostles by the Lord, we understand that their relationship must be solidified in the most viable way. It is done through personal encounters between the Lord and His Apostles, since they must build a relationship that gives them both confidence in one another. They must discover the strength and vulnerability of each other, if they are going to move beyond a master/servant relationship and into a more endearing friendship. For Apostles, this means they must endure the harshest of circumstances in their grooming. Yet, for the Lord, it means that he must continue to successfully bring these mighty officers through the fires of every circumstance they encounter, as he prepares them for the specific Kingdom assignment they will be entrusted to execute.

"Therefore, I take pleasure in infirmities, in reproaches, in necessities, in persecutions, in distress for Christ's sake: for when I am weak, then am I strong." (II Corinthians 12:10)

By the time Apostles receive their specific commission from the Lord, they no longer define themselves as being citizens of this earthly realm, as they now see they have nothing in common with this world. These officers have no problem upholding their citizenship in the heavenly realm and declaring their full allegiance to the Lord Jesus Christ because they understand the benefits attached to such a commitment. In fact, all that the Lord has is made accessible to His Apostles, as he will withhold no good thing from them. For this reason, there are no secrets concerning the Kingdom that are off limits to these mighty officers of the Lord. If they are to successfully establish His Kingdom on earth, they must understand it in every aspect.

"He answered and said unto them, because it is given unto you to know the mysteries of the kingdom of heaven, but to them it is not given." (Matthew 13:11)

Knowing that such officers would need to have unrestricted access to the Kingdom is the reason the Lord's prerequisite for Apostles is utter death to the flesh nature. He echoed this truth to the disciples, so they would understand the depths of their commitment to their God and His Kingdom. When viewing this truth from the perspective of the Lord, we see that he was dealing with a two-fold work. Yes, he was in the process of qualifying the disciples to eventually become Apostles, but he was also safeguarding the Kingdom of God from the possibility of corruption, as the enemies of God will never inherit or possess his regal, glorious, and eternal domain.

"Now this I say, brethren, that flesh and blood cannot inherit the kingdom of God; neither doth corruption inherit incorruption." (I Corinthians 15:50)

The Lord never kept the truth of the Kingdom silent from the disciples nor did he conceal from them the qualifications of entering the Kingdom. They were well informed on all fronts of what was necessary and inevitable to reach dominion in the Kingdom.

"And that we must through much tribulation enter into the kingdom of God." (Acts 14:22)

He made sure they were not blindsided by anything that the flesh, Satan, or the world threw at them in efforts to prevent them from entering or possessing the Kingdom. Yet, the Lord also knew that at times they would become weary in executing the duties of such high caliber officers. For this reason, he had no reservations about sharing in depth details with them about their Kingdom status. In fact, he used revelation as the driving force to keep them forging ahead even in the most unpleasant and unwelcoming circumstances.

"And Jesus said unto them, Verily I say unto you, that ye which have followed me, in the regeneration when the Son of man shall sit in the throne of his glory, ye also shall sit upon twelve thrones, judging the twelve tribes of Israel. And everyone that hath forsaken houses, or brethren, or sisters, or father, or mother, or wife, or children, or lands, for my name's sake, shall receive a hundredfold, and shall inherit everlasting life. " (Matthew 19: 28)

The Lord Jesus Christ knew that he only had a short span of three years to groom and equip His Apostles for the work that was set before them. Therefore, he made sure that they had a clear understanding of his road to glory because they too would have to walk the path that was paved by his life. Every Apostle knows that their journey will not be easy, but they are confident in the fact that it will be worth every step they take with the Lord and for the Lord. *"Yea doubtless, and I count all things* but *loss for the excellency of the knowledge of Christ Jesus my Lord: for whom I have suffered the loss of all things, and do count them* but *dung, that I may win Christ, And be found in him, not having mine own righteousness, which is of the law, but that which is through the faith of Christ, the righteousness which is of God by faith: That I may know him, and the power of his resurrection, and the fellowship of his sufferings, being made conformable unto his death; If by any means I might attain unto the resurrection of the dead. Not as though I had already attained, either were already perfect: but I follow after, if that I may apprehend that for which also, I am apprehended of Christ Jesus. Brethren, I count not myself to have apprehended:* but this one thing I do, *forgetting those things which are behind, and reaching forth unto those things which are before, I press toward the mark for the prize of the high calling of God in Christ Jesus. "* (Philippians 3:9-14)

ABOUT THE AUTHOR

Cynthia Alvarez is a dedicated servant of the Lord Jesus Christ. Her passion for the King and his Kingdom is undeniable as she continues to empower the Body of Christ in this hour. The goal of her work is to break believers out of the typical church pattern by acclimating them to the culture of the Kingdom of God. *'Apostles'* is nothing less than remarkable and life altering in every way. It is one of several books written by Cynthia Alvarez that is designed to transform lives and produce a harvest of souls that are qualified for dominion in the Kingdom of our eternal Lord and Savior Jesus Christ.

A special thanks to all who have supported the endeavors of Cynthia Alvarez with your purchase of this book. May the blessings of our Lord Jesus Christ richly increase you above measure.

Cynthia Alvarez

ABOUT THE BOOK

Apostles is a nothing less than astonishing as it gives readers an impressive scope of the Chief Kingdom Officer of the Lord God. It brings the Apostles to the forefront of the Lord's plans and actions in this earthly realm. It will arouse your appetite for the manifestation of the Kingdom of God, as He begins to reveal His mighty end-time Apostles in this hour. This book will cause the many hidden Apostles of God to come forth and take their rightful places as His mighty officers in this hour. Lives will be transformed by receiving insight into the broad spectrum of His Apostles as well as the significance of their accomplishments in the Kingdom of God. It is time for every Apostle of the Lord God to rise and be counted. You can no longer remain in obscurity or in silence. You must rise now and take the lead in the Kingdom of God.

Apostles was written for people everywhere who know there is more that God has ordained for them to do in this life. They know that God has called them to change the world in their lifetime. Without question, you will be empowered to do great and mighty things for the Lord God after reading this book. Your life will never be the same again!

Apostles

Cynthia Alvarez

Prophets

Cynthia Alvarez

Lightning Source UK Ltd.
Milton Keynes UK
UKHW022201260219

338052UK00009B/285/P

9 781945 698972